EMMANUEL JOSEPH

Global Jurisdiction, Navigating International Law

Copyright © 2025 by Emmanuel Joseph

All rights reserved. No part of this publication may be reproduced, stored or transmitted in any form or by any means, electronic, mechanical, photocopying, recording, scanning, or otherwise without written permission from the publisher. It is illegal to copy this book, post it to a website, or distribute it by any other means without permission.

First edition

This book was professionally typeset on Reedsy.
Find out more at reedsy.com

Contents

1	Chapter 1: The Foundations of International Law	1
2	Chapter 2: Sovereignty and Non-Intervention	3
3	Chapter 3: Human Rights and International Law	5
4	Chapter 4: The Law of Armed Conflict	7
5	Chapter 5: International Economic Law	9
6	Chapter 6: Environmental Law and Global Governance	11
7	Chapter 7: The Law of the Sea	13
8	Chapter 8: International Criminal Law	15
9	Chapter 9: International Organizations and Global Governance	17
10	Chapter 10: International Trade Law	21
11	Chapter 11: International Humanitarian Law and Armed...	23
12	Chapter 12: The Future of International Law	25

1

Chapter 1: The Foundations of International Law

International law serves as the backbone of the international community, governing the relationships between states and international organizations. At its core, international law is composed of a set of rules and principles that guide the behavior of states in their interactions with one another. These laws are derived from treaties, customary international law, general principles of law recognized by civilized nations, and judicial decisions and scholarly writings. The development of international law has been a dynamic process, influenced by historical events, cultural interactions, and the evolving needs of the global community.

The historical evolution of international law can be traced back to ancient civilizations, where early forms of diplomacy and treaties were practiced. However, it was not until the 17th century, with the emergence of the Westphalian system, that the concept of sovereign states and the principles of territorial integrity and non-intervention became foundational elements of international law. The Peace of Westphalia, signed in 1648, marked a turning point in the development of international legal principles, establishing the framework for modern state sovereignty and the recognition of states as equal actors in the international arena.

Customary international law, which consists of practices that have evolved over time and are accepted as binding, plays a significant role in shaping international legal norms. These customs are often based on the consistent and general practice of states, accompanied by a sense of legal obligation. For example, the principle of diplomatic immunity, which protects diplomats from legal actions in the host country, has its roots in customary international law. Additionally, the prohibition of genocide and torture are recognized as customary international laws that bind all states, regardless of whether they have ratified specific treaties.

Treaties, also known as conventions or agreements, are formal, written instruments that establish legal obligations between states. These binding agreements can address a wide range of issues, from human rights and environmental protection to trade and security. Treaties play a crucial role in the codification of international law, providing clarity and predictability in the relationships between states. The United Nations, established in 1945, serves as a central platform for the negotiation and adoption of international treaties, fostering cooperation and dialogue among member states.

The role of international courts and tribunals is essential in interpreting and enforcing international law. Institutions such as the International Court of Justice (ICJ) and the International Criminal Court (ICC) provide mechanisms for resolving disputes and holding individuals accountable for violations of international law. These judicial bodies contribute to the development of international legal norms by delivering authoritative interpretations and establishing precedents. The decisions of international courts not only resolve specific cases but also shape the broader understanding and application of international law.

2

Chapter 2: Sovereignty and Non-Intervention

The principles of sovereignty and non-intervention form the bedrock of international law, encapsulating the rights and duties of states within the global order. Sovereignty, at its core, refers to the supreme authority of a state to govern itself without external interference. This concept has evolved over centuries, gaining prominence in the aftermath of the Peace of Westphalia. Sovereignty is not merely about control over territory; it also encompasses the ability of states to enact laws, conduct foreign policy, and enter into international agreements as independent actors.

The principle of non-intervention reinforces the idea of sovereignty by prohibiting states from interfering in the internal affairs of other states. This principle is enshrined in the United Nations Charter, which emphasizes the importance of respecting the territorial integrity and political independence of all member states. Non-intervention serves as a safeguard against external coercion and ensures that states have the autonomy to manage their domestic affairs, including political, economic, and social matters, without unwarranted influence from other countries.

Despite its significance, the principle of non-intervention is not absolute. There are circumstances under which intervention may be deemed necessary and justified under international law. Humanitarian intervention, for instance, is often invoked in situations where gross human rights violations occur, such as genocide, ethnic cleansing, and crimes against humanity. In such cases, the international community may intervene to protect vulnerable populations and restore peace and security. The Responsibility to Protect (R2P) doctrine, endorsed by the United Nations, underscores the obligation of states and the international community to prevent and respond to mass atrocities.

The tension between sovereignty and intervention is a recurring theme in international relations. On one hand, states fiercely guard their sovereignty and resist any attempts at external interference. On the other hand, the need to address global challenges, such as human rights abuses, terrorism, and environmental degradation, often necessitates collective action and cooperation. Striking a balance between respecting state sovereignty and upholding international norms and values remains a complex and delicate task.

International institutions and mechanisms play a crucial role in mediating disputes and facilitating dialogue between states. The United Nations, through its various organs and agencies, provides a platform for states to discuss and address issues of common concern. The Security Council, in particular, has the mandate to maintain international peace and security, and it can authorize interventions in situations that threaten global stability. Regional organizations, such as the African Union and the European Union, also contribute to conflict resolution and peacebuilding efforts, demonstrating the importance of collaborative approaches in navigating the complexities of international law.

3

Chapter 3: Human Rights and International Law

Human rights are a cornerstone of international law, embodying the fundamental freedoms and protections to which all individuals are entitled. The Universal Declaration of Human Rights (UDHR), adopted by the United Nations General Assembly in 1948, serves as a landmark document that enshrines these rights. The UDHR outlines a comprehensive set of civil, political, economic, social, and cultural rights, establishing a universal standard for human dignity. It has inspired numerous international treaties, regional agreements, and national constitutions aimed at safeguarding human rights.

The protection and promotion of human rights are essential for fostering global peace and stability. International human rights law provides mechanisms for holding states accountable for human rights violations. Treaties such as the International Covenant on Civil and Political Rights (ICCPR) and the International Covenant on Economic, Social, and Cultural Rights (ICESCR) impose legal obligations on states to respect, protect, and fulfill human rights. These treaties are monitored by various United Nations committees, which review state compliance and provide recommendations for improvement.

Regional human rights systems play a crucial role in complementing international efforts. The European Court of Human Rights, the Inter-American Court of Human Rights, and the African Court on Human and Peoples' Rights are examples of regional institutions that adjudicate human rights cases and provide remedies for victims. These courts have developed a rich body of jurisprudence that contributes to the evolving understanding of human rights norms and principles. They also serve as important forums for individuals and groups seeking justice and redress for human rights abuses.

Non-governmental organizations (NGOs) and civil society actors are vital in advocating for human rights and holding governments accountable. Organizations such as Amnesty International, Human Rights Watch, and local human rights groups conduct research, document abuses, and campaign for justice. Their efforts often bring attention to issues that might otherwise be overlooked, exerting pressure on states to uphold their human rights obligations. The collaboration between international organizations, regional bodies, and civil society is essential for advancing the global human rights agenda.

Despite significant progress, challenges to human rights protection persist. Issues such as discrimination, inequality, armed conflict, and authoritarianism continue to undermine human rights in various parts of the world. The international community must remain vigilant and proactive in addressing these challenges, ensuring that human rights are respected and upheld for all individuals. Efforts to strengthen international human rights mechanisms, promote accountability, and support grassroots movements are critical in realizing the vision of a just and equitable world.

4

Chapter 4: The Law of Armed Conflict

The law of armed conflict, also known as international humanitarian law (IHL), governs the conduct of hostilities and seeks to mitigate the suffering caused by war. IHL is rooted in principles that aim to protect those who are not or no longer participating in hostilities, such as civilians, medical personnel, and prisoners of war. It also regulates the means and methods of warfare, prohibiting the use of weapons and tactics that cause unnecessary suffering or fail to distinguish between combatants and non-combatants.

The Geneva Conventions, adopted in 1949 and supplemented by Additional Protocols in 1977, are the cornerstone of IHL. These treaties establish comprehensive rules for the protection of victims of armed conflicts, including the wounded and sick, shipwrecked soldiers, prisoners of war, and civilians. The conventions also set out the responsibilities of occupying powers and provide mechanisms for the implementation and enforcement of IHL. States parties to the Geneva Conventions are required to disseminate the rules of IHL and ensure that their armed forces are trained to comply with these standards.

One of the key principles of IHL is the distinction between combatants and non-combatants. This principle mandates that parties to a conflict must at all times differentiate between those who are actively participating in hostilities and those who are not. Attacks must be directed solely at military objectives, and indiscriminate attacks that harm civilians are prohibited. Another fundamental principle is proportionality, which requires that the anticipated military advantage of an attack must outweigh the potential harm to civilians and civilian objects. The principle of necessity further stipulates that the use of force must be limited to what is necessary to achieve a legitimate military objective.

Enforcing IHL and holding violators accountable remains a significant challenge. The International Criminal Court (ICC) and other international tribunals play a critical role in prosecuting individuals responsible for war crimes, crimes against humanity, and genocide. These judicial bodies contribute to the development of IHL by delivering judgments that clarify legal standards and establish precedents. National courts also have a responsibility to investigate and prosecute serious violations of IHL, reinforcing the principle of complementarity, which ensures that justice is served at both the international and domestic levels.

The role of humanitarian organizations, such as the International Committee of the Red Cross (ICRC), is indispensable in the implementation and promotion of IHL. The ICRC works to protect and assist victims of armed conflicts, visiting detainees, providing medical care, and facilitating the exchange of information between separated families. The organization also engages in dialogue with parties to conflicts, advocating for compliance with IHL and raising awareness about the humanitarian impact of war. The collective efforts of states, international institutions, and humanitarian actors are essential in upholding the principles of IHL and alleviating the suffering caused by armed conflicts.

5

Chapter 5: International Economic Law

International economic law encompasses the rules and principles that govern economic relations between states and other actors in the global economy. It covers a wide range of areas, including trade, investment, finance, and development. The objective of international economic law is to promote economic cooperation, facilitate cross-border transactions, and ensure a stable and predictable environment for economic activities. It seeks to balance the interests of states, investors, and other stakeholders, fostering an inclusive and sustainable global economy.

The World Trade Organization (WTO) is a central institution in international economic law, responsible for regulating international trade and resolving trade disputes. The WTO's agreements, such as the General Agreement on Tariffs and Trade (GATT) and the General Agreement on Trade in Services (GATS), establish rules for market access, non-discrimination, and trade liberalization. The WTO's dispute settlement mechanism provides a forum for resolving trade conflicts, ensuring that member states adhere to their commitments and obligations. Through its work, the WTO contributes to a more open and transparent global trading system.

International investment law governs the protection and regulation of foreign investments. Bilateral investment treaties (BITs) and multilateral agreements, such as the International Centre for Settlement of Investment Disputes (ICSID) Convention, provide legal frameworks for the treatment of foreign investors. These agreements typically include provisions on fair and equitable treatment, protection against expropriation, and dispute resolution mechanisms. Investment arbitration, conducted by institutions such as ICSID, allows investors to seek redress for breaches of investment agreements, promoting investor confidence and stability in the investment environment.

Global financial regulation is another critical aspect of international economic law. Institutions such as the International Monetary Fund (IMF) and the World Bank play a key role in overseeing financial stability and providing financial assistance to countries in need. The IMF's mandate includes monitoring exchange rates, balance of payments, and macroeconomic policies, while the World Bank focuses on development financing and poverty reduction. These institutions work to prevent financial crises, support economic reforms, and promote sustainable development, contributing to the stability and resilience of the global financial system.

Development cooperation and international aid are essential components of international economic law. The United Nations' Sustainable Development Goals (SDGs) provide a comprehensive framework for addressing global challenges, such as poverty, inequality, and environmental degradation. International development agencies, donor countries, and multilateral organizations work together to provide financial resources, technical assistance, and capacity-building support to developing countries. Through these efforts, international economic law seeks to foster inclusive growth, reduce disparities, and achieve sustainable development for all.

6

Chapter 6: Environmental Law and Global Governance

Environmental law is a critical area of international law that addresses the protection and preservation of the natural environment. As the world grapples with challenges such as climate change, biodiversity loss, and pollution, international environmental law provides a framework for collective action and cooperation. Key treaties, such as the Paris Agreement on climate change, the Convention on Biological Diversity (CBD), and the Basel Convention on hazardous wastes, establish legal obligations for states to protect the environment and promote sustainable development.

The Paris Agreement, adopted in 2015, is a landmark treaty that seeks to limit global warming to well below 2 degrees Celsius above pre-industrial levels. It sets out commitments for states to reduce greenhouse gas emissions, enhance adaptive capacity, and mobilize financial resources for climate action. The agreement operates on a principle of common but differentiated responsibilities, recognizing that developed and developing countries have different capabilities and responsibilities in addressing climate change. Through nationally determined contributions (NDCs), states outline their specific plans and targets for mitigating climate change.

Biodiversity conservation is another critical aspect of international environmental law. The Convention on Biological Diversity (CBD), adopted in 1992, aims to conserve biological diversity, promote sustainable use of its components, and ensure fair and equitable sharing of benefits arising from genetic resources. The CBD establishes mechanisms for protecting ecosystems, habitats, and species, and it encourages states to integrate biodiversity considerations into national policies and strategies. The Nagoya Protocol, a supplementary agreement to the CBD, provides guidelines for access to genetic resources and the sharing of benefits from their use.

International environmental law also addresses the management of hazardous substances and wastes. The Basel Convention on the Control of Transboundary Movements of Hazardous Wastes and Their Disposal regulates the international trade and disposal of hazardous wastes, aiming to protect human health and the environment. The convention establishes requirements for prior informed consent, environmentally sound management, and the prevention of illegal trafficking of hazardous wastes. It is complemented by other treaties, such as the Rotterdam Convention on chemicals and pesticides and the Stockholm Convention on persistent organic pollutants.

Global governance mechanisms play a crucial role in coordinating and implementing environmental law. The United Nations Environment Programme (UNEP) serves as the leading global environmental authority, providing leadership, advocacy, and technical assistance to promote sustainable development. Multilateral environmental agreements (MEAs) establish institutional frameworks for monitoring compliance, facilitating cooperation, and addressing emerging environmental issues. Collaborative efforts between states, international organizations, civil society, and the private sector are essential for advancing environmental protection and achieving global sustainability goals.

7

Chapter 7: The Law of the Sea

The law of the sea is a specialized area of international law that governs the rights and responsibilities of states in maritime spaces. The United Nations Convention on the Law of the Sea (UNCLOS), adopted in 1982, is the primary legal instrument that establishes the legal framework for the use and management of the world's oceans and seas. UNCLOS sets out rules for the delimitation of maritime boundaries, the rights and duties of coastal and landlocked states, and the protection of the marine environment.

UNCLOS recognizes different maritime zones, each with specific legal regimes. The territorial sea extends up to 12 nautical miles from a state's coastline, where the coastal state exercises sovereignty over the waters, airspace, seabed, and subsoil. The contiguous zone, which extends up to 24 nautical miles from the baseline, allows the coastal state to enforce laws related to customs, immigration, and pollution. The exclusive economic zone (EEZ), extending up to 200 nautical miles, grants coastal states sovereign rights over the exploration and exploitation of natural resources in the water column and seabed.

One of the key principles of the law of the sea is the freedom of navigation, which allows ships of all states to navigate through international waters without interference. This principle is essential for facilitating international trade and ensuring the open and accessible nature of the oceans. However, states also have responsibilities to protect the marine environment and prevent pollution from ships, fishing activities, and other sources. UNCLOS includes provisions for the conservation and sustainable use of marine living resources, as well as measures to address marine pollution and preserve biodiversity.

Dispute resolution mechanisms under UNCLOS provide a framework for resolving conflicts between states over maritime issues. The International Tribunal for the Law of the Sea (ITLOS), the International Court of Justice (ICJ), and arbitral tribunals play a crucial role in interpreting and applying the provisions of UNCLOS. These judicial bodies ensure that disputes are resolved peacefully and in accordance with international law, contributing to the stability and predictability of the maritime legal order.

Regional cooperation is also vital for addressing maritime challenges and promoting sustainable ocean governance. Regional fisheries management organizations (RFMOs) play a significant role in regulating fishing activities and conserving fish stocks in specific geographic areas. Regional seas programs, coordinated by UNEP, facilitate cooperation among neighboring countries to address shared environmental issues and promote the sustainable use of marine and coastal resources. Through these collaborative efforts, states can work together to protect the health and productivity of the oceans for present and future generations.

8

Chapter 8: International Criminal Law

International criminal law is a branch of international law that deals with the prosecution and punishment of individuals responsible for serious crimes of international concern. These crimes include genocide, war crimes, crimes against humanity, and the crime of aggression. The goal of international criminal law is to hold perpetrators accountable, provide justice for victims, and deter future atrocities. It operates on the principle that individuals, regardless of their official capacity, can be held criminally liable for their actions.

The establishment of the International Criminal Court (ICC) in 2002 marked a significant milestone in the development of international criminal law. The ICC is a permanent, independent judicial institution with jurisdiction over the most serious international crimes. It operates based on the Rome Statute, which defines the crimes within its jurisdiction and outlines the procedures for investigation, prosecution, and trial. The ICC's mandate is to complement national judicial systems, intervening only when states are unwilling or unable to prosecute offenders.

The crime of genocide, defined by the Genocide Convention of 1948, involves acts committed with the intent to destroy, in whole or in part, a national, ethnical, racial, or religious group. Genocide includes acts such as killing, causing serious bodily or mental harm, and deliberately inflicting conditions calculated to bring about the group's destruction. The prosecution of genocide is crucial for preventing and addressing the most egregious violations of human rights and ensuring that perpetrators are brought to justice.

War crimes encompass serious violations of the laws and customs of war, including the targeting of civilians, the mistreatment of prisoners of war, and the destruction of civilian property. These crimes are defined in various international treaties, including the Geneva Conventions and their Additional Protocols. The prosecution of war crimes is essential for upholding the principles of international humanitarian law and ensuring accountability for violations committed during armed conflicts.

Crimes against humanity refer to widespread or systematic attacks directed against civilian populations, including acts such as murder, torture, enslavement, and forced displacement. Unlike war crimes, crimes against humanity can occur during both armed conflict and peacetime. The prosecution of these crimes is critical for addressing large-scale abuses of human rights and providing justice for victims. The crime of aggression, defined by the Rome Statute, involves the use of armed force by a state against the sovereignty, territorial integrity, or political independence of another state. The prosecution of the crime of aggression aims to deter unlawful military actions and promote international peace and security.

9

Chapter 9: International Organizations and Global Governance

International organizations play a vital role in the governance of the global community, providing platforms for cooperation, dialogue, and collective action. These organizations, which include the United Nations (UN), the World Health Organization (WHO), and the International Monetary Fund (IMF), facilitate the implementation of international law, promote development, and address global challenges. They operate based on principles of multilateralism, where states work together to achieve common goals and address issues that transcend national borders.

The United Nations, established in 1945, is the principal international organization dedicated to maintaining international peace and security, promoting human rights, and fostering social and economic development. The UN's Charter serves as the foundational legal document that outlines the organization's purposes, principles, and structure. The UN General Assembly, composed of all member states, provides a forum for discussion and decision-making on a wide range of issues. The Security Council, with its mandate to address threats to peace, has the authority to adopt binding resolutions and authorize collective measures, including the use of force.

Specialized agencies and programs of the UN, such as the WHO, the United Nations Children's Fund (UNICEF), and the United Nations Development

Programme (UNDP), focus on specific areas of international cooperation. The WHO, for example, plays a critical role in coordinating global health initiatives, responding to public health emergencies, and setting international health standards. UNICEF works to protect the rights of children and promote their well-being, while the UNDP supports sustainable development and poverty reduction efforts in developing countries.

International financial institutions, such as the IMF and the World Bank, are essential for promoting economic stability and development. The IMF provides financial assistance and policy advice to countries facing balance of payments problems, while the World Bank offers funding and technical support for development projects. These institutions work to foster economic growth, reduce poverty, and promote global financial stability. Their efforts are complemented by regional development banks, such as the African Development Bank and the Asian Development Bank, which address specific regional needs and priorities.

Non-state actors, including non-governmental organizations (NGOs), multinational corporations, and civil society groups, also play a significant role in global governance. NGOs, such as Oxfam and Greenpeace, advocate for social justice, environmental protection, and human rights, often influencing international policy and decision-making. Multinational corporations impact global economic trends and contribute to international development through investment, innovation, and corporate social responsibility. Civil society groups, including grassroots organizations and social movements, engage in advocacy, awareness-raising, and

continue

International organizations play a vital role in the governance of the global community, providing platforms for cooperation, dialogue, and collective action. These organizations, which include the United Nations (UN), the World Health Organization (WHO), and the International Monetary Fund (IMF), facilitate the implementation of international law, promote development, and address global challenges. They operate based on principles of multilateralism, where states work together to achieve common goals and address issues that transcend national borders.

CHAPTER 9: INTERNATIONAL ORGANIZATIONS AND GLOBAL GOVERNANCE

The United Nations, established in 1945, is the principal international organization dedicated to maintaining international peace and security, promoting human rights, and fostering social and economic development. The UN's Charter serves as the foundational legal document that outlines the organization's purposes, principles, and structure. The UN General Assembly, composed of all member states, provides a forum for discussion and decision-making on a wide range of issues. The Security Council, with its mandate to address threats to peace, has the authority to adopt binding resolutions and authorize collective measures, including the use of force.

Specialized agencies and programs of the UN, such as the WHO, the United Nations Children's Fund (UNICEF), and the United Nations Development Programme (UNDP), focus on specific areas of international cooperation. The WHO, for example, plays a critical role in coordinating global health initiatives, responding to public health emergencies, and setting international health standards. UNICEF works to protect the rights of children and promote their well-being, while the UNDP supports sustainable development and poverty reduction efforts in developing countries.

International financial institutions, such as the IMF and the World Bank, are essential for promoting economic stability and development. The IMF provides financial assistance and policy advice to countries facing balance of payments problems, while the World Bank offers funding and technical support for development projects. These institutions work to foster economic growth, reduce poverty, and promote global financial stability. Their efforts are complemented by regional development banks, such as the African Development Bank and the Asian Development Bank, which address specific regional needs and priorities.

Non-state actors, including non-governmental organizations (NGOs), multinational corporations, and civil society groups, also play a significant role in global governance. NGOs, such as Oxfam and Greenpeace, advocate for social justice, environmental protection, and human rights, often influencing international policy and decision-making. Multinational corporations impact global economic trends and contribute to international development through investment, innovation, and corporate social responsibility. Civil society groups, including grassroots organizations and social movements, engage in advocacy, awareness-raising, and community mobilization, driving positive change at the local, national, and international levels.

10

Chapter 10: International Trade Law

International trade law governs the rules and practices that facilitate the exchange of goods and services across borders. It aims to create a fair and predictable trading system that promotes economic growth, development, and cooperation among states. The World Trade Organization (WTO) is the primary institution responsible for regulating international trade, providing a framework for trade negotiations, dispute resolution, and the enforcement of trade agreements.

The WTO operates based on a set of principles that guide international trade relations. These principles include non-discrimination, which ensures that countries do not favor one trading partner over another and provide the same treatment to all WTO members. The principle of most-favored-nation (MFN) treatment requires that any trade advantage granted to one country must be extended to all other WTO members. The principle of national treatment mandates that imported goods and services should be treated no less favorably than domestic products once they have entered the market.

Trade liberalization is a key objective of the WTO, aiming to reduce trade barriers such as tariffs, quotas, and subsidies. Through successive rounds of negotiations, WTO members have agreed to lower tariffs on a wide range of products, facilitating greater market access and competition. The General Agreement on Tariffs and Trade (GATT), which predates the WTO, serves as the foundation for these negotiations, establishing rules for the reduction of tariffs and other trade barriers. The WTO also oversees trade in services through the General Agreement on Trade in Services (GATS) and intellectual property rights through the Agreement on Trade-Related Aspects of Intellectual Property Rights (TRIPS).

The WTO's dispute settlement mechanism provides a structured process for resolving trade disputes between member states. When disputes arise, countries can bring their cases to the WTO's Dispute Settlement Body, which establishes panels to examine the issues and make rulings. The Appellate Body reviews appeals and ensures that the legal interpretations are consistent with WTO agreements. This mechanism helps maintain the stability and predictability of the global trading system, ensuring that trade rules are enforced and respected.

Regional trade agreements (RTAs) and free trade agreements (FTAs) complement the multilateral trading system by promoting trade liberalization and economic integration at the regional level. Examples include the North American Free Trade Agreement (NAFTA), the European Union (EU) Single Market, and the African Continental Free Trade Area (AfCFTA). These agreements often go beyond WTO commitments, addressing issues such as investment, competition, and labor standards. They enhance economic cooperation among member states and contribute to the overall growth of international trade.

11

Chapter 11: International Humanitarian Law and Armed Conflicts

International humanitarian law (IHL), also known as the law of armed conflict, seeks to mitigate the humanitarian consequences of war by regulating the conduct of hostilities and protecting those who are not or no longer participating in the conflict. IHL is based on principles of humanity, distinction, proportionality, and military necessity, aiming to limit the suffering caused by armed conflicts and ensure respect for human dignity.

The Geneva Conventions of 1949 and their Additional Protocols of 1977 form the core of IHL, establishing comprehensive rules for the protection of victims of armed conflicts. The conventions address various categories of individuals, including the wounded and sick in armed forces, shipwrecked sailors, prisoners of war, and civilians. They also outline the responsibilities of occupying powers and set standards for the humane treatment of detainees. The International Committee of the Red Cross (ICRC) plays a crucial role in promoting and implementing IHL, providing humanitarian assistance, monitoring compliance, and advocating for the protection of victims.

One of the fundamental principles of IHL is the distinction between combatants and non-combatants. Parties to a conflict must at all times differentiate between those who are actively participating in hostilities and those who are not. Attacks must be directed solely at military objectives, and indiscriminate attacks that harm civilians are prohibited. Another key principle is proportionality, which requires that the anticipated military advantage of an attack must outweigh the potential harm to civilians and civilian objects. The principle of necessity further stipulates that the use of force must be limited to what is necessary to achieve a legitimate military objective.

The enforcement of IHL and accountability for violations are essential for upholding the rule of law in armed conflicts. The International Criminal Court (ICC) and other international tribunals, such as the International Criminal Tribunal for the former Yugoslavia (ICTY) and the International Criminal Tribunal for Rwanda (ICTR), prosecute individuals responsible for war crimes, crimes against humanity, and genocide. These judicial bodies contribute to the development of IHL by delivering judgments that clarify legal standards and establish precedents. National courts also have a responsibility to investigate and prosecute serious violations of IHL, reinforcing the principle of complementarity.

Humanitarian organizations, including the ICRC and Médecins Sans Frontières (MSF), play a vital role in providing assistance and protection to victims of armed conflicts. They operate in conflict zones, delivering medical care, food, water, and shelter to those in need. These organizations also engage in advocacy and awareness-raising, highlighting the humanitarian impact of conflicts and calling for greater respect for IHL. The collective efforts of states, international institutions, and humanitarian actors are essential in ensuring the effective implementation of IHL and alleviating the suffering caused by war.

12

Chapter 12: The Future of International Law

As the world continues to evolve, so too must international law adapt to address emerging challenges and opportunities. Technological advancements, globalization, and shifting geopolitical dynamics present both opportunities and complexities for the international legal system. The future of international law will be shaped by the ability of the global community to navigate these changes and uphold the principles of justice, equality, and cooperation.

One of the key areas of focus for the future of international law is the regulation of emerging technologies. Innovations in fields such as artificial intelligence, biotechnology, and cybersecurity raise new legal and ethical questions that require international cooperation and governance. Developing legal frameworks that address issues such as data privacy, intellectual property, and the responsible use of technology will be crucial for ensuring that technological advancements benefit all of humanity.

Climate change and environmental sustainability will continue to be critical issues for international law. Strengthening global environmental agreements, enhancing climate action, and promoting sustainable development are essential for addressing the urgent threats posed by climate change. The international community must work together to implement the commitments made under the Paris Agreement and other environmental treaties, ensuring that all countries contribute to a sustainable and resilient future.

Human rights and social justice will remain central to the future of international law. Ensuring the protection of human rights in an increasingly interconnected world requires continuous efforts to strengthen legal mechanisms, promote accountability, and address inequalities. International human rights law must evolve to address new challenges, such as digital rights, migration, and the impact of economic globalization on vulnerable populations. The international community must remain committed to advancing human rights and social justice for all individuals, regardless of their nationality, race, gender, or socioeconomic status.

The future of international trade and economic law will be shaped by the need to balance economic growth with social and environmental considerations. As global trade and investment continue to expand, international economic law must address issues such as fair trade, sustainable development, and corporate social responsibility. Strengthening the multilateral trading system, promoting inclusive economic policies, and ensuring that the benefits of globalization are shared equitably will be essential for fostering a just and prosperous global economy.

International cooperation and multilateralism will be critical for addressing global challenges and promoting peace and security. Strengthening the Emerging legal issues, such as the regulation of outer space, the use of autonomous weapons, and the governance of artificial intelligence, will also shape the future of international law. Developing legal frameworks that address these complex and rapidly evolving areas will be essential for ensuring that technological advancements are used responsibly and ethically. The international community must engage in proactive and forward-looking dialogue to anticipate and address these challenges.

The future of international law will also be influenced by the evolving geopolitical landscape. Shifts in global power dynamics, regional conflicts, and changes in political leadership can impact the development and implementation of international legal norms. Ensuring that international law remains relevant and effective in a changing world requires adaptability,

CHAPTER 12: THE FUTURE OF INTERNATIONAL LAW

resilience, and a commitment to upholding the rule of law.

In conclusion, the future of international law holds both challenges and opportunities. By fostering cooperation, embracing innovation, and upholding the principles of justice and equality, the international community can navigate the complexities of the modern world and build a more just, peaceful, and sustainable global order.

Global Jurisdiction: Navigating International Law

In an increasingly interconnected world, the need to understand and navigate the complexities of international law has never been more crucial. "Global Jurisdiction: Navigating International Law" offers an insightful exploration into the multifaceted world of international legal principles and their application. This comprehensive book delves into the foundational aspects of international law, including sovereignty, non-intervention, human rights, and the law of armed conflict, providing readers with a thorough understanding of these critical concepts.

The book begins by examining the historical development and sources of international law, setting the stage for a deeper exploration of contemporary issues. Readers will gain insights into the intricacies of human rights protection, the regulation of armed conflict, and the role of international courts and tribunals in enforcing legal norms. The chapters on international economic law and environmental law highlight the interplay between legal frameworks and global challenges, offering perspectives on trade, investment, and sustainable development.

"Global Jurisdiction" also addresses the evolving nature of international law in the face of emerging technologies, climate change, and shifting geopolitical dynamics. It underscores the importance of international cooperation and multilateralism in addressing transnational threats and fostering global peace and security. Through its comprehensive coverage and engaging narrative, this book serves as an indispensable resource for students, practitioners, and anyone interested in the dynamic field of international law.

Embark on a journey through the landscape of global jurisdiction and discover how international law shapes our world, resolves conflicts, and promotes justice and equity on a global scale.

www.ingramcontent.com/pod-product-compliance
Lightning Source LLC
LaVergne TN
LVHW020742090526
838202LV00057BA/6178